The Big, Ginormous Book of Clean Jokes and Riddles
By Thomas Mercaldo

Copyright © 2017 Thomas Mercaldo

All rights reserved. No part of this book may be reproduced in any form or by any electronic mechanical means, including information storage and retrieval systems, without permission in writing from the publisher, except by reviewers, who may quote brief passages in a review.

Editing by Bethany Pereira
Cover artwork by Heather Schnabel
Typesetting by Devon Slattery
Book Design by Dylan Bartel

Printed and bound in U.S.A.
First Printing 2017

Published by Aquinas Eagle Publishing, a division of Aquinas Scout Books
154 Herbert Street,
Milford, CT 06461

Table of Contents

Early Favorites 4
Elephants 22
Planes, Trains, and Automobiles 37
    Planes 39
    Trains 42
    Automobiles 47
Under the Sea 54
In the Forest 67
    Deer 75
At the Zoo 77
Out of this World 86
On the Farm 96
Perfect Timing 106
Fun With Numbers 119
Play That Music 131
Did You Hear About…? 144
Final Favorites 153

Early Favorites

What happened to the skydiver whose parachute didn't open?

He jumped to a conclusion.

What is the first thing you need to achieve a goal?
A soccer ball.

Why doesn't the Statue of Liberty tell knock-knock jokes?
Freedom rings.

What do Alexander the Great and Kermit the Frog have in common?
The same middle name.

Where can you go that is so quiet you can hear a pin drop?
A bowling alley.

What do you call a scared flower arranger?
A petrified florist.

What did the out of shape burglar risk when being chased by the police?
Cardiac arrest.

Where did the first corn come from?
The stalk brought it.

What do you call two guys hanging on a window?
Kurt and Rod (curtain rod).

How do prisoners call each other?
They use cell phones.

What happened when the devil burned down the shoe store?
A thousand soles were lost.

What do Martin Luther King, Christopher Columbus, and Abraham Lincoln all have in common?
They were all born on holidays.

Who invented the first airplane that couldn't fly?
The Wrong Brothers.

Why are sports arenas always so windy?
There are so many fans in there.

What bow can't be tied?
A rainbow.

What do you call the children of a stupid florist?
Blooming idiots.

What word becomes shorter when you add two letters to it?
Short.

What do you call a yo-yo with no string?
A no-yo.

What do you call a sad strawberry?
A blueberry.

What kind of monkey can fly?
A hot air baboon.

Where were the first French fries made?
In grease (Greece).

What happens when you forget to pay the exorcist?
You get repossessed.

What do people in Canada call little black cats?
Kittens.

How did the student make straight A's?
He used a ruler.

What did the bald man say when he got a comb for Christmas?
I'll never part with it.

What is the mass of one cubic yard of oriental soup?
Won ton (one ton).

How much should a neutron pay for his electric bill?
For neutrons, there is no charge.

What do frogs in Paris eat with their hamburgers?
French flies.

What's it called when a prisoner takes a picture of himself?
  A cell-fie.

What happens when an owl contracts laryngitis?
  He no longer gives a hoot.

Why did the robber take a bath?
  He wanted a clean get away.

If April showers bring May flowers, then what do Mayflowers bring?
  Pilgrims.

What word is always pronounced incorrectly?
  Incorrectly.

Who did Antarctica marry?
Uncle Arctica.

What happened to the woman who fell into the upholstery machine?
She's fully recovered.

Why did the man name both of his sons Ed?
Two Eds are better than one.

Why did the cross-eyed teacher get fired?
She couldn't control her pupils.

If you're being chased in a circle by 42 horses, what should you do?
Get off the merry-go-round.

Why shouldn't you advertise for your lost cat?
Cats can't read.

What do you always find in the middle of nowhere?
The letter "h".

Why were there so many problems for the dentist who married a manicurist?
They fought tooth and nail.

What do mice do during the daytime?
Mouse-work.

What has four legs and catches flies?
Two outfielders.

What happened to the cat that swallowed a ball of yarn?
　　She had mittens.

What school did Sherlock Holmes graduate from?
　　Elementary, my dear Watson.

What's the main ingredient in Lassie's dog biscuits?
　　Collie flour.

What do liars do when they die?
　　Lie still.

What do you call a cloistered priest eating potato chips?
A chip monk.

Why should a golfer wear two pairs of pants?
In case he makes a hole in one.

Did you hear about the man who fell into the lens grinding machine?
He made a spectacle of himself.

During the annual Marine-Navy basketball game, all of the Marine's starters fouled out. Who did the coach put in?
The sub-marines.

What do you call a teacher that never says your name right?
Miss Pronounce.

Why was the robot never afraid?
He had nerves of steel.

What do snowmen eat for breakfast?
Frosted flakes.

Why did Miss Muffet need a GPS?
She lost her whey.

What's the opposite of a hurricane?
A him-icane.

What did one hot dog say to another?
Hi, Frank.

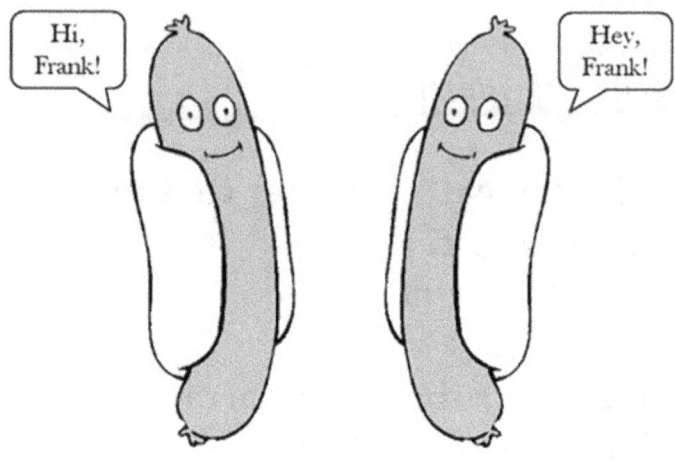

Boss: Didn't you tell me you were leaving to go see the dentist yesterday?
Worker: Yes, I did.
Boss: Then why did I see you and one of your friends walking out of a basketball game?
Worker: Well, my friend is a dentist, and I saw him at the game.

John: Look sis, I bought two new packs of cards and put them together to make one pack of cards.
Jane: Big deal.

A man with a strawberry growing out of his head goes to the doctor. The doctor says, "Let me give you some cream to put on that."

A snail walked into a bank to make a deposit. Suddenly, a turtle busted in and robbed the bank. When the police finally arrived, they interviewed the snail and asked him to recount what had happened.
Traumatized, the snail answered, "I don't know. It all happened so fast."

Two pirates, Red Beard and Black Beard, meet on the dock. Black Beard has a patch over one eye, a hook for a hand, and a wooden leg. "Me gads, matey," says Red Beard. "Whatever happened to ya?"

Black Beard stammers, "Me pirate ship was attacked, and a lucky shot took off me leg. So now I got me a wooden peg leg."

"And what about yer hand?" asks Red Beard.

"Well, when me ship sank, a shark bit off me hand. So now I got meself a hook."

"Arrg, that's terrible! Now, how did ya get that eye patch?"

"I was standin' on a dock, and the biggest, nastiest seagull I ever saw poops right in me eye!"

"That's bad luck, but ya don't go blind from bird poop."

"Well," says Black Beard, "The thing was, it was me first day with the hook."

What kind of bank account does a mouse have?

A Swiss account.

Elephants

Why didn't the elephant want to use a computer?

He was afraid of the mouse.

Why do elephants wear green sneakers?
So they can hide in the tall grass.

Why shouldn't you go in the jungle between 2 and 4 pm?
Because the elephants are swinging from tree to tree.

Why are pigmies so small?
They go into the jungle between 2 and 4 pm.

Why do elephants hide behind trees.
So they can trip ants.

How do you know if an elephant has been in the jungle?
You see a lot of tripped ants.

Why do some elephants' tusks stick out?
They couldn't afford braces.

A gray, long-eared African Elephant married a brown, small-eared Indian Elephant. What type of animal was their first born?

An elephant.

What's the difference between an African Elephant and an Indian Elephant?

About 3,000 miles.

What's the difference between elephants and grapes?

Grapes are purple.

What did the elephants say when they saw Tarzan coming over the hill?
Here comes Tarzan coming over the hill.

What did the elephants say when they saw Tarzan coming over the hill wearing sun glasses?
Nothing, they didn't recognize him.

What did Jane say when she saw the elephants coming over the hill?
Here come the grapes! (Jane was color-blind.)

What did the grape say when the elephant stepped on it?
Nothing. It just let out a little wine.

Why do elephants paint their toenails red, green, yellow, and pink?
So they can hide in the jellybean jar.

Have you ever seen an elephant hiding in the jellybean jar?
Works, doesn't it?

What do you find between elephants' toes?
Slow running natives.

How do you make an elephant float?
Two scoops of ice cream, a can of soda, and some elephant.

Where do Indian Elephants go for sandwiches?
To New Deli.

What is gray, has four legs, and a trunk?
A mouse going away on vacation.

What weighs over one ton, has four legs, and flies?
A dead elephant.

What do you get when you cross an elephant with a groundhog?
Very big holes in your backyard.

What's gray and goes up and down, up and down?
An elephant stuck in an elevator.

Why don't young elephants bring backpacks to camp?
They keep everything in their trunks.

Why do elephants turn around in circles three times before bed?
One good turn deserves another.

How do you get an elephant out of a box of Jell-O?
Follow the directions on the box.

Why did the elephant lie down in the middle of the road?
To stop the chicken from crossing.

Why are elephants large, gray, and wrinkly?
If they were small, round, and white, they would be Aspirins.

How do you stop an elephant from charging?
Take away his credit card.

What do you call a hitch-hiking elephant?
A two ton pickup.

Why do elephants have trunks?
They can't fit everything in their glove compartments.

What can you say about nine elephants wearing pink pajamas and one elephant wearing blue pajamas?
Nine out of ten elephants prefer pink pajamas.

Why aren't elephants allowed on public beaches?
They can't keep their trunks up.

Why do ducks have webbed feet?
To stamp out forest fires.

Why do elephants have flat feet?
To stamp out burning ducks.

What's gray and stamps out forest fires?
Smokey the Elephant.

What do you do with a green elephant?
Wait until it ripens.

What do you do with a blue elephant?
Cheer it up.

What's gray and comes in a red and white can?
Cream of elephant soup.

What is green and has a trunk?
A seasick tourist.

Why are elephants so wrinkled?
It takes too long to iron them.

How is an elephant like a banana?
They're both grey, except for the banana.

How do you shoot a blue elephant?
With a Blue Elephant Gun.

How do you shoot a white elephant?
Hold its trunk until it turns blue, and then shoot it with a Blue Elephant Gun.

How do you find big elephants?
Pretty easily.

But, where do you find big elephants?
Wherever you left them.

Why do elephants prefer peanuts to steak?
They're easier to get at the ballpark.

What's gray and cheers you up when you are sick?
A get well-ephant.

What's gray, beautiful, and wears one glass slipper?
Cinder-elephant.

What do elephants do for laughs?
They tell people jokes.

What's the difference between an elephant and a lemon?
A lemon is yellow.

Which animals were the last to leave the ark?
The elephants – they stayed to pack their trunks.

An elephant and a giraffe walk kdown to the watering hole for a drink. They spot a turtle fast asleep, basking in the sun. The elephant runs over and kicks the turtle – wack- to the other side of the shore.

"Oh boy, that was cruel!" said the giraffe.

The elephant said, "That turtle bit a chunk out of my trunk fifty years ago."

"Fifty years ago? Wow, what a great memory," said the giraffe.

"Yes," said the elephant, "I have turtle recall."

Why do elephants prefer peanuts to steak?
 They're easier to get at the ballpark.

What's gray and cheers you up when you are sick?
 A get well-ephant.

What's gray, beautiful, and wears one glass slipper?
 Cinder-elephant.

What do elephants do for laughs?
 They tell people jokes.

What's the difference between an elephant and a lemon?
 A lemon is yellow.

Which animals were the last to leave the ark?
 The elephants – they stayed to pack their trunks.

An elephant and a giraffe walk kdown to the watering hole for a drink. They spot a turtle fast asleep, basking in the sun. The elephant runs over and kicks the turtle – wack- to the other side of the shore.

"Oh boy, that was cruel!" said the giraffe.

The elephant said, "That turtle bit a chunk out of my trunk fifty years ago."

"Fifty years ago? Wow, what a great memory," said the giraffe.

"Yes," said the elephant, "I have turtle recall."

My friend bought me an elephant and put it in my room. I said, "Thank you." He said, "Don't mention it."

Hickory Dickory Dock,
The elephant ran up the clock.
The clock is now being repaired.

It was a boring afternoon, so the Ants decided to challenge the Elephants to a game of soccer. The game was going well, with the Ants beating the Elephants five to zero. The Ants once again gained possession, and their star player was dribbling the ball towards the Elephants' goal when the Elephants' fullback came lumbering towards the ant. The elephant stepped on the little ant, killing him instantly.

The referee blew his whistle and stopped the game. "What do you think you're doing? That's poor sportsmanship – killing another player."

The elephant replied, "Well, I didn't mean to kill him – I was just trying to trip him up."

Planes, Trains, and Automobiles

What do you call an airplane that crashes?

An error-plane.

Planes

Why was the airline pilot angry?
He wasn't angry. He just had a bad attitude.

What happened to the pilot who flew into a 4,000 lb hamburger?
He was grounded.

How often do airplanes crash?
Usually just once.

Why was Peter Pan on the no fly list?
If he were onboard, the plane would Never-Never-Land.

Why did the boy study on the airplane?
He wanted a higher education.

What is the day before an airplane crashes?
Mayday.

What do you get when you cross a dog and an Irish airplane?
A jet setter.

What do you call it when you're sick of waiting for your plane?
Terminal illness.

Which part of the plane is the laziest?
The wheels. They're always tired.

> Two wrongs don't make a right, but two Wrights made an airplane.

> A good landing is one you walk away from, but a great landing is one where you can re-use the equipment.

"Don't fly this plane any faster than the speed of sound," said the old lady to the captain.

"Why's that?" the captain laughed.

The old woman looked at him and said, "Because my friend and I want to talk, that's why."

Trains

Why don't elephants like riding on trains?
They hate leaving their trunks in the baggage car.

Why couldn't the engineer be electrocuted?
He's not a conductor.

What's as big as a train, but weighs absolutely nothing?
The train's shadow?

How did the locomotive learn to run on the tracks?
It trained for it.

Why can't a steam locomotive sit down?
It has a tender behind.

John: (after crossing a set of train tracks) Hey, a train just went by!
Jack: How do you know?
John: It left its tracks.

How do you find a missing train?
You follow its tracks.

How do locomotives hear?
Through the engineers.

What's the difference between a train and a teacher?
A train goes "Choo-Choo," but a teacher tells you to go spit your gum out.

What happened to the man that took the 5 o'clock train home?
He had to give it back.

What happened to the boy that walked along the train tracks?
He felt run down.

What do trains do with food?
Chew, Chew.

Ticket inspectors. You've got to hand it to them...

If an electric train travels 90 miles per hour in a western direction, and the wind is blowing at 5 miles per hour from the north, which direction will the smoke be blowing?

There's no smoke. It's an electric train.

Joe, Jim and Bob all went camping for the first time. While they were walking, they kept finding different types of tracks. Joe found the first set and proudly announced, "Look! I found rabbit tracks."

Then, Jim found a second set and told his friends, "Look! I found fox tracks."

Bob found yet another set, but had no clue what animal could have made these tracks. In confusion he called out to the other two, "Hey, what kind of tracks are these?" Then a train hit him…

A man woke up in a panic as he was going to be late to work again. He called the taxi company and said, "Can you please help me? I need a taxi now. I have to get on the 10 o'clock to New York!"

The man from the taxi service responded, "I'm sorry sir, we are very busy at the moment, but we will send someone out as soon as a taxi opens up. Don't worry too much though, the 10 o'clock to New York is always late."

"And it's going to be extra late today," the man sighed. "I'm the engineer."

Automobiles

Should you take your car out in a storm?
 Only if it's a driving rain.

How do frogs start their cars when they won't turn over?
 By jump starting them.

What happened to the man who bought snow tires for his car?
 They melted before he even got home.

What ten-letter word starts with gas?
 Automobile.

How did the car get a flat tire?
 There was a fork in the road.

What did the tornado say to the sports car?
 Ready to go for a spin?

If people in America only drove white cars, what would the country become?
> A white car-nation.

What would you call it if everyone in America went back to living in their cars?
> A case of re-in-car-nation.

When is a car not a car?
> When it turns into a driveway.

What kind of melody do you sing while driving?
> A car tune (cartoon).

What do you get when the motor of a car goes up in flames?
> A fire engine.

Did you hear about the hospital that makes cars go faster?
> Apparently, they give cars a fuel injection.

Did you hear about the new car that runs on peanut butter?
The only problem is they stick to the roof of the garage.

Did you hear about the new tires that are filled with diet soda instead of air?
The only problem is if you leave them out for too long, the tires get flat.

Did you hear about the new car that runs on grapes?
The only problem is sometimes it makes the engine wine.

Did you hear about the new car that runs on prunes?
The only problem is it has to make too many pit stops.

Why is an old car like a baby?
It never goes anywhere without a rattle.

What do you get when you merge your pet with your car?
A car-pet.

What do you get when you cross a mummy and a car mechanic?
Toot and Car Man.

What should you take if you feel run down?
The license plate of the car that hit you.

What's the first thing a ghost does when it gets into the front seat of a car?
Fastens the sheet belt.

Why did the stupid race car driver make 10 pit stops at the Indianapolis 500?
He kept asking for directions.

> My sista bet me that I couldn't make a car out of spaghetti, so she was shocked when I drove pasta.

A boy drove home after passing his driving test and drove the car right into the living room. "How did you manage to do that?" his father fumed.

"Simple, Dad. I came in through the kitchen and turned left."

Once there was a snail who was sick of being slow. So, he went to a car dealership, ordered a really fast sports car, and asked the dealer to paint a big "S" on each side of the car. Now, whenever people see that snail zooming along in his new car, they look and say, "Hey, look at that S-car go!"

An American farmer visited a small farm in Poland. The proud Polish farmer showed off his farm. "This is where I grow lettuce, tomatoes, and cucumbers," he beamed. "Here is where I grow beans, corn, and potatoes."

The land was tiny, and the American was surprised by its small size. "Is this all of your land?" he asked.

"Yes," the Polish farmer said proudly. "This is all mine!"

"You mean this is it? This is all of it?" the American said incredulously.

"Yes, yes! This is really all mine!"

"Well," said the American, "back in America, I could get in my car before the sun came up and I'd drive and drive and drive and when the sun set, I'd still only be halfway across my farm!"

"Oh, yes," replied the Polish farmer with a grin. "I used to have a car like that too."

Joe got careless with matches and lit the field behind his house on fire. Thinking quickly, he ran into the house and called the fire department.

"The field is on fire," Joe cried into the phone.

"Calm down," the dispatcher intoned. "Now how do we get to the field?"

"Don't you still have that red truck?" Joe inquired.

Under the Sea

What do you get from an angry shark?

You get as far away as possible.

How do you communicate with fish?
You drop them a line.

Why are oysters so greedy?
They're shellfish.

Did you hear about the ship filled with yo-yos bound for New York that got caught in a violent storm?
It sank 25 times.

What lies at the bottom of the ocean and quivers?
A nervous wreck.

What's the easiest way to catch a fish?
Have someone toss it to you.

What kind of money lender breaks legs and eats fish?
A loan shark.

Why are fish so smart?
They live in schools.

What do you call a fish that has two knees?
A two-knee fish.

Which fish is the most famous?
The star-fish.

What happens when you throw a blue stone into the Red Sea?
The stone gets wet.

What did the lobster bring to his teacher?
A crab apple.

What puts the white lines in the ocean?
An ocean liner.

What happened when a ship carrying red paint crashed into a ship carrying purple paint?
Both crews were marooned.

Why did the fish play video games all day?
He was hooked.

Did you hear about what happened to the fish that showed up late for work?
He was canned.

How do you keep a fish from smelling?
Cut off its nose.

Why are some fish at the bottom of the ocean?
They dropped out of school.

How do you close a letter underwater?
With a seal.

How come fish always know their weight?
They have scales.

Why don't dolphins play tennis?
They're afraid of the net.

What kind of sandwiches do baby dolphins like?

Peanut butter and jellyfish sandwiches.

What's the difference between a fish and a piano?

You can tune a piano, but you can't tuna fish.

How did the seagull hurt himself while eating a clam?

He pulled a mussel.

Why did the lobster feel crummy?

He was hanging out with a bunch of crabs.

Do dolphins ever do anything by accident?
No. They do everything on porpoise.

What do you get for a fish that can't hear?
A herring aid.

Why don't fish do well in school?
They're all below C level.

What sort of fish performs surgical operations?
A sturgeon.

What would happen if you threw a million books into the ocean?
There would be a title wave.

Why were the sea horses singing in the reef?
They were in a coral group.

What happened when the fried fish got into a fight?
A bunch of fish were battered.

Why was the pelican in debt?
He had a very large bill.

What fish can make your piano sound great?
A tuna.

Why did the dolphin cross the road?
To get to the other tide.

What country do dolphins prefer?
Finland.

Why couldn't the sailors play cards?
The captain was standing on deck.

Why did the captain grab a bar of soap as his ship was sinking?
He thought he would wash up on shore.

Where do boats go when they are sick?
To the dock.

What kind of ship does Dracula sail?
A blood vessel.

What lives in the ocean and agrees with you?
A seal of approval.

What did the captain do when the boy leaned over the back of the boat?
He gave him a stern look.

What do you call a boy floating on a raft in the sea?
Bob.

What do fish say when they run into a concrete wall?
Dam!

What's stranger than seeing a catfish?
Seeing a goldfish bowl.

Why do seagulls fly over the sea?
If they flew over the bay, they would be bay-gulls (bagels).

What's yellow and drives passengers along the ocean floor?
A taxi crab.

Why do crabs only like salt water?
Pepper water makes them sneeze.

> If you think of a better fish pun, please let minnow.

Two goldfish are in a tank together. One says to the other, "Do you know how to drive this thing?"

Two trout were dining in a restaurant and they finished their waters. After waiting a frustratingly long amount of time without any service, one trout began waving his glass in the air. The waiter finally saw him, turned to the busboy, and said, "There are two fish out of water at table 5."

In the Forest

What do you call a brown bear wearing earmuffs?

Anything you want. He can't hear you.

Why are teddy bears never hungry?
   They're always stuffed.

What's smarter than a talking dog?
   A spelling bee.

What kind of gum do bees chew?
   Bumble gum.

Why do bees itch?
   They have hives.

What did the bee say when he returned to the hive?
   Honey, I'm home.

What kind of bee is difficult to understand?
   A mumble bee.

What kind of bee trips a lot?
   A stumble bee.

Why was the insect thrown out of the forest?
He was a litter bug.

What kind of tree can fit in one hand?
A palm tree.

Which forest animal eats with its tail?
All of them. None of them remove their tail to eat.

What kind of socks do bears wear?
None. They have bear feet.

What kind of bear likes to be in the rain?
A drizzly bear.

Why was the mother firefly unhappy?
Her children weren't very bright.

How do you catch a squirrel?
By climbing up a tree and acting like a nut.

What's a tree's least favorite month?
Sep-timber.

How do trees check their emails?
They log on.

How do you tell if a tree is a dogwood?
From the bark.

What stories do giant sequoia trees tell?
Tall tales.

Why did it take the giraffe so long to apologize?
It took a long time for him to swallow his pride.

What has a yellow stomach and sucks sap from trees?
A yellow-bellied sap sucker.

What do you call a bear with no teeth?
A gummy bear.

What do you call a snake who works for the government?
A civil serpent.

What do trees do when part of their company shuts down?
They start a new branch.

Why was the mother owl worried about her son?

He didn't give a hoot about anything.

What do possums have that no other animal has?

Baby possums.

What do you call a black bear at the North Pole?

Lost.

Which pine has the sharpest needles?

A porcu-pine.

Why couldn't the snake talk?
It had a frog in its throat.

What did the father buffalo say to his son when he was leaving the reservation?
Bye, son (bison).

What do you call a lizard that tells jokes?
A stand up chameleon.

Deer

What do you call a deer with no eyes?
No eye deer.

What do you call a deer with no eyes and no legs?
Still no eye deer.

Where do you find a deer with no legs?
Right where you left it.

Who did Bambi invite to his birthday party?
His deer-est friends.

Why do male deer need braces?
They have buck teeth.

What did the impatient stag say to his wife?
Hurry up, deer.

What do you get when you cross Bambi with a ghost?
Bamboo.

At the Zoo

Bob: I'd like some crocodile shoes please.

Joe: All right then, what size is your crocodile?

How do you keep a rhinoceros from charging?
Take away his cell phone cord.

Why shouldn't you play cards in the jungle?
Too many cheetahs.

What's a crocodile's favorite drink?
Gator-ade.

What happened when the lion ate the clown?
He felt funny.

How many different types of gnus are in Africa?
Two. Good gnus and bad gnus.

Which side of a cheetah has the most spots?
The outside.

A zebra with wide stripes married a zebra with narrow stripes. Their first son had no stripes. What did they call him?
Harold.

What fruit do baby apes like to sleep in?
Ape-ri-cots (Apricots).

What do you call a hippopotamus that gets angry when others steal food from him, but then steals food from others?
A hippo-crite.

How do you make sure a hippopotamus is telling you the truth?
Make him take the Hippocratic Oath.

Which animal can jump higher than a tree?
All of them. Trees can't jump.

What do you get when you cross a panther and a Doberman?
One terrified mailman.

Why wouldn't the leopard take a bath?
He didn't want to become spotless.

What did the leopard say after it started to rain on a hot summer day?
That really hits the spots.

Why do flamingos stand on one leg?
If they lifted both legs, they would fall over.

What did the banana say to the monkey?
Nothing. Bananas can't talk.

Why do gorillas have such large nostrils?
They have very large fingers.

Why are the apes in America so noisy?
They were raised in a zoo.

Which animal is helpful with laundry?
A clothes lion.

Who won the race between the cheetah and gazelle?
The gazelle won because cheetahs never win.

Why didn't the lion want to eat the antelope?
He was tired of eating fast food every night.

What do you call vandalism done by a long-necked animal?
Giraffiti.

How does a polite lion greet his fellow animals?
Hello, pleased to eat you.

What do you call a monkey in a minefield?
A baBOOM!

> My friend was trying to irritate me with bird puns, but I realized that toucan play at that game.

Why do bears wear fur coats?
They would look strange if they wore jackets.

Why do giraffes have long necks?
Their feet smell.

> Get me a crocodile sandwich, and make it snappy!

Why is it hard for a leopard to hide in the jungle?
They're always spotted.

Once upon a time, a beautiful, young antelope had a wild date in the jungle. She got all gussied up and put on her new dress. Suddenly, as she was just about ready, she was stampeded by a herd of wildebeests. She became the world's first self-dressed, stamped antelope.

A duck, a skunk, and a deer went out for dinner at a fancy restaurant one night. When it came time to pay for the dinner, the skunk didn't have a scent, and the deer didn't have a buck, so they put the check on the duck's bill.

Out of this World

Have you heard about the first cow astronaut?

He landed on the moooooon.

Why did the astronauts find bones on the moon?
The first cow didn't make it.

Why didn't the astronauts stay on the moon?
When they arrived, the moon was full.

Why do astronauts blast off at noon?
12 o'clock is time for launch.

What did the astronomer say when he was asked if he liked shooting stars?
No comet.

How many balls of string would it take to reach the moon?
Just one if it's long enough.

How did the rocket lose his job?
He was fired.

What do they call the signal lights cowboys place on their saddles for night round-ups?
Communication saddle lights.

What happened to the astronaut that stepped in chewing gum?
He was stuck in Orbit.

How did the alien hold up his pants?
With an asteroid belt.

How do you have a good solar system party?
You planet (plan it).

Why did Mickey Mouse take a trip to outer space?
He was looking for Pluto.

What did the astronaut say to the author?
I took your book into orbit and I couldn't put it down.

How do you put a baby astronaut to sleep?
You rock it (rocket).

What do you call a wizard from outer space?
A flying sorcerer.

What do you call an alien with four eyes?
An aliiiien.

Why did the moon stop eating?
It was full.

What kind of plates do they use in space?
Flying saucers.

Why didn't the sun go to college?
It already had a million degrees.

What only works after it's been fired?
A rocket.

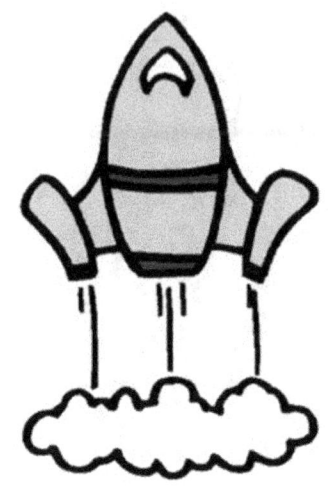

What did Mars say to Saturn?
Give me a ring sometime.

Where does an astronaut keep their sandwich?
In a launch box.

What is heavier: a full moon or a half-moon?
The half-moon because the full moon is lighter.

But, when is the moon the heaviest?
When it's full.

If athletes get athlete's foot, what do astronauts get?
Missile toe.

Joe and Jack took a trip to Maine and were camping under the stars. As they gazed at the sky, Jack wondered aloud, "Do you think the moon or Florida is further from right here?"

"Are you seriously asking that?" Joe snapped. "Isn't the answer obvious? I'll give you a hint. We can't see Florida from here, can we?"

Two astronauts were in a spaceship circling the moon. While one slept, the other decided to go on a spacewalk. After floating outside and taking in the view, he tried to get back in the ship, but realized the cabin door had locked. He knocked on the cabin door, but there was no answer. He knocked louder, but still nothing. Scared of being stuck floating in space forever, he pounded on the door with all of his strength until he got a response. From inside he heard a terrified voice call out, "W-w-w-who's there?"

I would tell you another joke about space, but it's too out of this world!

What kind of knots are tied in space?
Astro-knots.

On the Farm

What do you call a cow who takes a nap at a construction site?

A bull dozer.

What do you write if you want to break up with your tractor?
A John Deere letter.

What did the police do when 200 hares escaped from a rabbit farm?
They combed the area.

How do you know carrots are good for your eyes?
You never see rabbits wearing glasses.

What animal wears shoes to bed?
Horses.

Why did the lettuce win the race?
It was a head.

What do you get from a pampered cow?
Spoiled milk.

What do you call it when chickens change nests?
An egg-change.

Geography Teacher: Where's Moscow?
Student: In the barn next to Pa's cow.

Why was the farmer mad?
Someone got his goat.

What do you call a chicken that doesn't look both ways before crossing the road?
Dead.

What did the farmer get when he crossed a chili pepper, a shovel, and a collie?
A hot-diggity-dog.

What's orange and sounds like a parrot?
A carrot.

How did the scarecrow win a Nobel Prize?
He was out standing in his field.

What did the farmer use to fix the hole in his jeans?
A cabbage patch.

What do you call a cow with a sense of humor?
A laughing stock.

What did the baby corn say to its mother?
Where's Pop-corn?

Why were the baby blueberries crying?
Their parents were in a jam.

What does a horse do when it is tired?
It hits the hay.

What happened to the baby chicken that misbehaved in school?
He was egg-spelled.

Why did the farmer take hay to bed?
He wanted to feed his night-mares.

What do farmers use to make crop circles?
Pro-tractors.

What do you call a dog with no legs?
It doesn't matter what you call him; he still isn't coming.

What should a pig do if he has a broken pigpen?
Use a pencil.

What do you call a cow with no legs?
Ground beef.

What do you call a cow with two legs?
Lean meat.

How do you know that owls are smarter than chickens?
Have you ever heard of Kentucky Fried Owl?

What did the farmer do when he lost his favorite cow?
He tractor-down.

What kind of horse only goes out at night?
A night-mare.

What do you put on a sunburned pig?
Oink-ment.

What did the farmer say when he lost his tractor?
Where's my tractor?

What do you call a cow that doesn't give milk?
An udder failure.

Why is it loud in the barn?
The cows have horns.

What did the cow say to the pig?
I'm afraid you're just a boar.

How did the pig feel when he lost his voice?
Disgruntled.

Why did the pony whisper?
He was a little horse (hoarse).

What do you call a pig that knows karate?
A pork chop.

What did the worm do in the cornfield?
He went in one ear and out the other.

On a farm, what grows when it's fed, but dies when it's watered?
A fire.

If fruit comes from fruit trees, then where do chickens come from?
Poul-trees.

Why did the farmer plant light bulbs?
He wanted to grow a power plant.

Why does a chicken coop have two doors?
If it had four doors, it would be a sedan.

A farmer is milking his cow. As he is milking, a fly comes along and flies into the cow's ear. A little bit later, the farmer notices the fly in the milk. The farmer says, "Hmph. In one ear, out the udder."

What animal is the best at Math?
Rabbits; they multiply very rapidly.

Perfect Timing

Why did the fool sell his alarm clock?

It kept going off when he was sleeping.

Why did the fool throw the clock out the window?
He wanted to see time fly.

If a woman gave a child five nickels and his brother 25 cents, what time would it be?
A quarter to two.

What are the odds of something happening at 12:50 pm?
Ten to one.

How many seconds are there in one year?
Twelve seconds. January 2nd, February 2nd, March 2nd...

It takes four minutes to hard boil one egg. How many minutes does it take to hard boil four eggs.
Four minutes.

What time is it when five leopards are chasing you?
Five after one.

Why should you never tell a secret near a clock?
Time will tell.

What type of dog keeps the best time?
A watchdog.

Why does time fly so fast?
People are always trying to kill it.

If your watch is broken, why can't you do your homework?
You don't have the time.

What's always behind time?
The back of a clock.

What's the best time to eat a banana?
When the moment is ripe.

What time is it when a pie is divided among four people?
A quarter to four.

What part of a clock is always old?
The second hand.

How long will a seven-day clock run without winding?
It won't run at all without winding.

What's a good way to kill time in the winter?
Sleigh it.

Why is there no such thing as a whole day?
Every day breaks.

If you smashed a clock, would you be accused of killing time?
Not if the clock struck first.

What time is the same forwards and backwards?
Noon.

What's the difference between a prison warden and a watchmaker?
One watches cells, and the other sells watches.

What time is it when a lion eats the Postmaster?
8 pm (Postmaster = PM).

When is the time of day like the whistle of a train?
Two to two.

How does a witch tell time?
With a witch watch.

What did the German clockmaker say to the clock that went tick, tick, tick, tick?
Ve haf vayys of making you tock.

What time is it when an elephant is sitting on your fence?
Time to get a new fence.

What time was it when the Italian broke his tooth?
Tooth-hurty (two thirty).

Why is a clock like a river?
It doesn't run long without winding.

Why was the clock scratching?
It had ticks.

What's another name for a grandfather clock?
An old timer.

What occurs once in every minute, twice in every moment, but not even once in one hundred thousand years?
The letter "m".

When the clock strikes thirteen, what time is it?
Time to get your clock fixed.

What did the digital clock say to its mother?
Look Ma, no hands.

Why is a clock like a condemned man?
Its hours are numbered.

Did you hear about the clock that went tick, tick, tick?
It was the tock of the town.

Did you hear that the man who invented the clock has written his autobiography?
Well, it's about time.

If a fly and a flea pass each other, what time is it?
Fly past flea.

My parrot swallowed a wristwatch.
Now all we ever hear is polly-ticks.

Did you hear about the thief that stole a calendar?

He got 12 months.

What time is it when three men are shoveling snow, and a fourth man is watching them?

Winter time.

What do you call a wristwatch born in the 25th century?

A future wrist tick.

What's the best time of year to use a trampoline?

Spring-time.

Joe: I woke up last night with the feeling that my watch was gone.
Bob: Was it gone?
Joe: No, but it was going.

Bob: This clock will run for 30 days without winding.
Jim: That's great! How long will it run if you wind it?

Joe: What time is it?
Bob: I don't know, but it's not 6 o'clock yet.
Joe: How do you know?
Bob: Because my mother said I need to be home before 6 o'clock. I'm not home yet, so it can't be 6 o'clock.

First Clock: I heard you broke your hand.
Second Clock: Yeah, but it's okay. I've got a second hand.

A jeweler was carrying a large grandfather clock to his shop for repairs. On his way along a crowded street, he accidentally ran into a lady and knocked her to the ground. "Why can't you just be like normal people, "yelled the woman, "and wear a watch?"

While proudly showing off his new apartment to friends, a college student led the way into the den. "What is the big brass gong and hammer for?" one of his friends asked. "That is the talking clock," the man replied. "How's it work?" the friend asked. "Watch," the student said, then proceeded to give the gong an ear shattering pound with the hammer. Suddenly someone screamed from the other side of the wall, "KNOCK IT OFF, YOU JERK! It's two AM!"

If 10 dogs run after 4 cats, what time is it?
10 after 4.

Fun With Numbers

What should you write on the tombstone of a mathematician?

What are 5 peaches plus 3 peaches? That's simple. Don't you know the answer? Haven't you ever done a problem like this in school?

No. In school, we only add apples.

Teacher: If you had 6 candy bars and I asked you for 3, how many would you have left?
Johnny: 6.
Teacher: Clever. Well, if I took 3 candy bars from you, then what would you have?
Johnny: 6 and no teacher.

What tool helps you with math?
Multi-pliers.

Do you say 6 plus 7 is 11, or 6 plus 7 are 11?
Neither. You say 6 plus 7 equals 13.

Two men were playing checkers. They played 5 games, and they each won the same number of games. How is this possible?

They were playing against different people.

If you had one million dollars and gave a quarter of it away, how much money would you have left?

$999,999.75.

Why didn't the two 4's feel like eating dinner?

They already 8.

What do you have if you have 6 pinions in one hand and 5 pinions in the other?

A difference of a pinion.

In mathematics, what's the law of the donut?

2 halves equal 1 hole (whole).

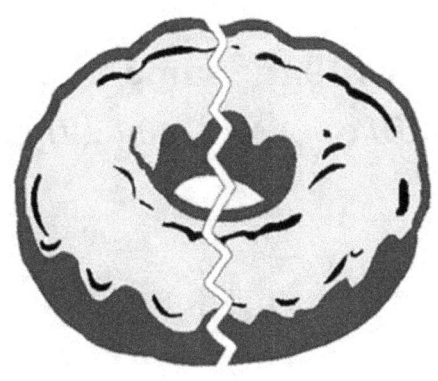

If there were 10 cats on a copy machine and 1 cat jumped off, how many cats were left?

None, because they were all copy cats.

What do you get when you divide the circumference of a Jack-O-Lantern by its diameter?

Pumpkin pi.

If 12 people make a dozen, how many make a million?

Very few people make a million.

What geometric figure represents a lost parrot?
   A polygon (Polly gone).

Why is 2 times 10 the same as 2 times 11?
   2 times 10 equals 20, and 2 times 11 equals twenty-too.

What does 5Q + 5Q equal?
   (10Q)
   You're welcome.

Why did the newspaper headline read 1 + 1 = 2?
   It was the first addition (edition).

If 1 is lonely, 2 is company, and 3 is a crowd, what are 4 and 5?
   9.

Jim bought 2 dozen donuts and all but 11 were eaten. How many donuts are left?
   11.

When a man faints, what number will revive him?
You must bring him 2.

What do you call a cat with 8 sides?
An octo-puss.

Why did the kitchen have trouble counting?
It's counter was broken.

Why is a horse with a lame leg like adding 6 and 7?
He puts down the three and carries one.

Which month has 28 days in it?
All of them have at least 28 days.

What did one math book say to the other?
Don't bother me, I've got my own problems.

Why did the math teacher give up teaching?
He had too many problems.

Why did the 20-dollar bill do so well in school?
It paid attention.

If you have 15 cows and 5 goats, what do you get?
A lot of milk.

Why didn't the dime roll down the hill with the penny?
It had more cents.

What are 2 and 4?
They're numbers.

Who invented fractions?
Henry the 1/8th.

I had a fight with 1, 3, 5, 7, and 9. The odds were against me.

What do you call a metric cookie?
A gram cracker.

What's the difference between an old penny and a new nickel?
4 cents.

If you have 3 apples and 8 oranges in your right hand, and 6 apples and 2 oranges in your left hand, what do you have?

Very large hands.

Joe: My dog is a mathematical genius!
Bob: How do you know?
Joe: I asked him, "How much is 5 minus 5?" He said nothing.

Billy: Excuse me, but I don't think that I deserve a zero on this quiz.
Teacher: Well, neither do I, but a zero is apparently the lowest score I can give you.

Teacher: Please recite your tables for me.
Billy: Kitchen table, dining room table, bedside table…

Billy: Would you punish a student for something they haven't done?
Teacher: No, I would never do that.
Billy: Oh good! I didn't do my math homework.

Why isn't your nose 12 inches long?
Then it would be a foot.

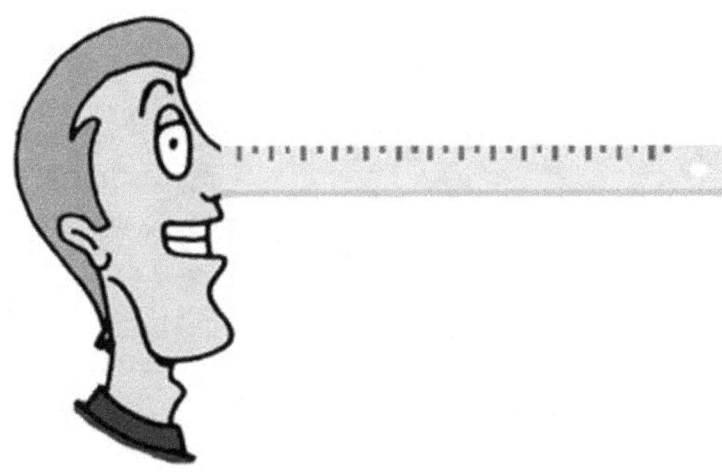

> Some people are afraid of heights, but not me. I'm afraid of widths.

Play That Music

How are trumpet players and pirates similar?

They're both murder on the high C's.

How do you make music stand?
Take the musicians' chairs away.

What's brown and lies on a piano bench?
Beethoven's last movement.

What happens when a band plays in a thunderstorm?
The conductor gets struck by lightning.

Did you hear about the bagpiper that played in tune?
Neither did I.

What has Beethoven been doing for the last 100 years?
De-composing.

What did the musician do when he lost the beat?
He had a tempo-tantrum.

Why wasn't the famous composer home?
He was out Chopin.

Why shouldn't you hit a famous composer?
They might hit you Bach.

What is the difference between 16 ounces of lead and a pianist?

The lead weighs a pound and the pianist pounds away.

What is the difference between a banjo and an onion?

Nobody cries when you chop up a banjo.

Why was the singer signed to a major league baseball contract?

They heard he had perfect pitch.

Why wasn't the band leader hurt after he was struck by lightning?

He was an excellent conductor.

How much wood is needed to build a piano?

At least one cord.

Why do bees hum?

They don't know the words.

What note don't bees like?
Bee-flat.

Which part of the body is the most musical?
Organs.

Why wasn't the train able to leave on time?
The conductor was with the orchestra.

Why did the girl strike piano keys with a pencil?
She was trying to write a song.

What was the first musical score?
8 to 4.

With whom does an elastic trumpet player play?
With a rubber band.

What has eight feet and sings?
A quartet.

What's the noblest instrument?
An upright piano.

How do musicians brush their teeth?
With a tuba toothpaste.

Why was the musician arrested?
For getting into treble.

What's Beethoven's favorite fruit?
Ba-na-na-naaaaa.

How do you know there's a singer at your door?
They can't find the key and they never know when to come in.

Do you want to hear a joke about a staccato?
Wait, that one's too short.

What kind of music do astronauts like?
Rocket roll.

Which bone can be used as an instrument?
The trom-bone.

Which part of a turkey can be used as an instrument?
The drumstick.

Which part of a snake is the most musical?
The scales.

What happened to the orchestra that played Beethoven?
They lost by a big score.

What's a balloon's least favorite type of music?
Pop.

What's a mummy's favorite type of music?
Rap.

Why was the piano locked out?
He lost all of his keys.

A drummer, sick of being bullied by her bandmates, decided that she was going to switch instruments.

She walked into the music store and pointed out the new instruments she would like to learn to play, saying, "I would like that trumpet and that accordion, please."

Extremely confused, the cashier responded, "Well, I guess I can sell you that fire extinguisher, but I think my boss would be really mad if I gave you the radiator."

Why couldn't anyone find the famous composer?
He was Haydn.

Did you hear about the musical ghost?
He wrote haunting melodies.

What do you get when you drop a piano down a mine shaft?
A-flat minor.

What do you say when you run over an army officer with a steam roller?
See, flat major.

What kind of soap do composers use to wash their hands?
Anti-Bach-terial.

Soloist 1: I once sang the Star Spangled Banner for six hours straight.
Soloist 2: That's nothing. I can sing the Stars and Stripes Forever.

Patient: Hey doc, I know this is going to be a pretty intense operation, but do you think I'll be able to play the piano when this is all over?
Doctor: Yes, of course you will.
Patient: Oh, that's awesome! I always wanted to be able to play the piano!

> B flat, G flat, and E flat walk into a bar. The bartender says, "Sorry, we don't serve minors."

Knock knock.
(Who's there?)
Little old lady.
(Little old lady who?)
Wow! You're so talented! I didn't realize you could yodel.

After practicing for a week, Joe decided it was time to perform a trumpet song for his friends. His friends cringed, covering their ears as he blasted wrong notes. When he finished, Joe asked, "So, is there anything else you guys would like me to play?"

"Yes!" Robby replied, "How about dominos instead?"

Why type of music do ghosts like?
Spirituals.

Why did the robot win the dance contest?
He was a dancing machine.

Did You Hear About...?

Did you ever see a horse fly?

Did you hear about the new doctor doll?
You wind it up and it operates on batteries.

Did you hear about the Big Bad Wolf doll?
You wind it up and it blows down your house.

Did you hear about the boy who plugged his electric blanket into the toaster?
He popped out of bed all night.

Did you hear about the man who named his horse Radish?

Did you hear about the dog that ate nothing but garlic?
His bark was much worse than his bite.

Did you hear about the invisible man who married an invisible woman?
Their kids aren't much to look at.

Did you hear about the two satellite dishes that got married?
The wedding was terrible, but the reception was great.

Did you hear about the man who lost his left arm and leg in a car accident?
He's all right now.

Did you hear about the new Dracula doll?
You put batteries in and it bites a Barbie Doll on the neck.

Did you hear about the man who got sacked from the calendar factory?
It was because he took a day off.

Did you ever see a shoe box?
What size gloves did it wear?

Did you hear about the new deodorant called "Vanish"?
You spray it on and you become invisible, so no one knows where the smell is coming from.

Did you hear about the man who works in the watch factory?
He just stands around and makes faces all day.

Did you hear about the broken change machine?
It doesn't make any cents.

Did you hear about the man that put on a clean pair of socks each day of the week?
By Friday, he could hardly get his shoes on.

Did you hear about the housewife who had a tiny kitchen?
It was so small she could only use condensed milk.

Did you hear about the burglar that fell into the cement mixer?
He's now a hardened criminal.

Did you hear about the new restaurant on the moon?
The food is great, but there's no atmosphere.

Did you hear about the robber that broke the laws of gravity?
He got a suspended sentence.

Did you hear about the girl who wasn't pretty and wasn't ugly?
She was pretty ugly.

Did you hear about the paranoid bloodhound?

He was convinced that certain people were following him.

Did you hear the joke about the limousine?

I'll tell you some other time. It's pretty long.

Did you hear about the bike that went around biting people because it was possessed by demons?
It was known as a vicious cycle.

Did you hear about the man who couldn't find a singing partner?
He ended up buying a duet-your-self kit.

Did you hear about the old lady who told knitting jokes?
You might say she was a real nit-wit.

Why didn't the boy get a license for his puppy?
The puppy was too young to drive.

Did you hear about the retired coin dealer?
All he does now is sit at home and talk about old dimes.

Did you hear about the dog that ran two miles just to get a stick?

You might say that story is a little far-fetched.

Have you ever seen a cat fish?

Final Favorites

What did the spider say to the annoying insect?
Stop bugging me.

What is black and says, "Pardon me," when it pushes its way out of the ground?
Refined oil.

Why did the robot act stupid?
He had a screw loose.

What do you call a skeleton that goes out in the snow without a coat or hat?
A numbskull.

What happened when the wheel was invented?
It created a revolution.

What did Leonardo DiCaprio wear to aerobics class?
A leo-tard.

Where can you find the Great Plains?
In the great airports.

What did the nut say as it was sneezing?
Ca-shew.

Why is the tooth fairy so smart?
She has a lot of wisdom teeth.

Who is the smartest monster?
Frank Einstein.

How was the crossword puzzle fan buried?
Six feet down and three feet across.

How did Benjamin Franklin discover electricity?
It came to him in a flash.

What do you call a sheepdog with the flu?
A germy shepherd.

Where do geologists go for entertainment?
Rock concerts.

If a boxer were knocked out by Dracula, what would he be?
Out for the count.

Why did the cyclops stop teaching?
He had only one pupil.

Why did the witch use Microsoft Word?
She wanted to use spell check.

How do rodents keep their breath fresh?
They use mouse-wash.

What did the picture say to the wall?
I've got you covered.

Why did the orange stop rolling down the hill?
It ran out of juice.

How do you make gold soup?
Use 14 carrots (karats).

Who makes suits and eats spinach?
Popeye the tailor man.

Did you hear about the stupid water polo player?
His horse drowned.

What type of cans are there in Mexico?
Mexi-cans.

What is a computer's first sign of old age?
Loss of memory.

What did the baby computer say to the Mommy computer?
I want my Da-ta.

How do you get rid of varnish?
Take away the "r".

What phrase is used to offer praise to a computer programmer?
Data boy.

What kind of bird jumps out of airplanes?
Parrot troopers.

When is a blue math book not a blue math book?
When it's read.

How many books can you fit in an empty library?
One. Then it is no longer empty.

What's the best way to pass a geometry test?
Know all of the angles.

What happened when Ray met a man-eating lizard?
He became ex-Ray (x-ray).

What subject are witches good at in school?
Spelling.

What was the largest island before Australia was discovered?
Australia.

In what country can you never win or lose?
Thailand (tie land).

What happens when business is slow at the medicine factory?
You can hear a cough drop.

Can you name the capital of every state in the union in 50 seconds?
Yes – Washington, D.C.!

Did you hear about the little boy who was named after his father?
They called him "Dad".

What are snowmen dances called?
Snowballs.

Why do barbers make good taxi drivers?
They know all the shortcuts.

Why did the teacher wear sunglasses to school?
Her students were very bright.

How did people react when electricity was first discovered?
Everyone was shocked.

Why was Cinderella thrown off the basketball team?
She kept running away from the ball.

What should you give your aunt for a sore throat?
Auntie-septic.

Why did the teacher run outside in the rain with her purse open?
She was expecting some change in the weather.

What happened when the cat swallowed a penny?
There was money in the kitty.

What do you get if you pour boiling water down a rabbit hole?
Hot cross bunnies.

I hear the invisible man is crazy.
You know what they say: out of sight, out of mind.

What did the computer programmer have for a snack?
Microchips.

A butcher is 6'1" and wears a size 11 shoe. What does he weigh?
> *Meat.*

How can you make a turtle fast?
> *Take away his food.*

What is a bacteria?
> *The back entrance to the cafeteria.*

Why doesn't Batman catch many fish?
> *Robin keeps eating all his worms.*

What do you call an alligator in a sweater vest?
> *An in-vest-a-gator.*

When did the Irish potato change nationalities?
> *When it became a French fry.*

Why does Batman brush his teeth so often?
> *To prevent bat breath.*

Why did the invisible man turn down a job offer?
He just couldn't see himself doing it.

Why couldn't the invisible boy see his mother or father?
They were transparents.

What bird is always out of breath?
A puffin.

Why did the girl bring a credit card to her teacher?
She wanted to get extra credit.

Why don't pterodactyls make noise when they use the bathroom?
Their "p" is silent.

Bob: I got a 100 in school today!
Mom: Really? That's great! In what subject?
Bob: I got a 50 in math and a 50 in history.

Mom: What was that loud noise?
Bob: My jacket fell on the floor.
Mom: Why would your jacket make such a loud noise?
Bob: I was wearing it.

Mom: Tell your sister that you're sorry for saying she's stupid.
Brother: I'm sorry you're stupid, sis.

Jim: You probably think I'm a perfect idiot.
Bob: No. I don't think you're perfect.

Mom: Did you eat all of the cookies in the cookie jar?
Bob: No, I didn't touch one.
Mom: Well, how come there is only one left?
Bob: That's the one I didn't touch.

Mom: How did you do on your report card?
Bob: The same as George Washington.
Mom: Well, how did he do?
Bob: He went down in history.

Sherlock and Watson decided to go camping, so they went into the woods, pitched their tents, caught and ate their dinner, and then laid down to sleep. Sherlock suddenly said, "Watson, look up and tell me what you deduce."

Watson responded, "Well I see hundreds of stars, but there are hundreds of millions of stars that I cannot see. Among those stars there are different planets which all create galaxies, and those galaxies make up solar systems, and those solar systems make up the universe. The universe is infinitely large from which I deduce that somewhere out there, there must be some other form of life."

"Interesting," Sherlock responded.

"Well, what do you deduce?" Watson inquired.

Sherlock sighed, "Someone stole our tents."

More Scout Fun Books Available at
Aquinaseagle.com

The Big Book of Camping Jokes and Riddles
140 Pages Filled with over 500 Jokes and Riddles related to camping and hiking. The perfect book to bring along to any Scouting event!

Scout Skits
A compilation of more than 75 campfire skits featuring traditional favorites and more modern variations. Fun for everyone!

Scout Riddles
Looking for a good laugh? Pull out a copy of Scout Riddles and you will be laughing immediately.

Campfire Tales
Filled with scary stories, humorous tales and Scouting legends.

Scout Jokes
One stop shop for the best jokes related to Scouting, camping and hiking.

Superior Campfires
Great guide to making any campfire memorable!

More Scout Skits
Do you need more skits? This book is filled with plenty to keep everyone entertained.

Run-ons and Even More Scout Skits
A collection of run-ons, walk-ons, one-liners and new skits.

Scout Cheers
Cheers to make any Scouting adventure that much more fun!

Scoutmaster's Minutes
A collection of thought-provoking readings and quotes.

Scoutmaster's Minutes II
Need more ways of inspiring your troops? More thought provoking readings and quotes inside.

Creative Campfires
The ultimate book for turning your ordinary campfire something extraordinary!

Collect Them All!
Scout Fun Books – Eagle Scout Gifts – Neckerchief Slides – Wood Badge Products – Motivational Products

www.ingramcontent.com/pod-product-compliance
Lightning Source LLC
Chambersburg PA
CBHW071401290426
44108CB00014B/1638